Escape the 9-5

"The Hustle & Grind of a Work from Home Recruiter"

By

Dale R Oran

otherwise, by any usage or abuse of any policies, processes, or directions contained within is the sole and utter responsibility of the recipient reader. Under no circumstances will any legal responsibility or blame be held against the publisher for any reparation, damages, or monetary loss due to the information herein, either directly or indirectly.

Respective authors own all copyrights not held by the publisher.

The information herein is offered for informational purposes solely and is universal as so. The presentation of the information is without a contract or any type of guarantee assurance.

The trademarks that are used are without any consent, and the publication of the trademark is without permission or backing by the trademark owner. All trademarks and brands within this book are for clarifying purposes only and are owned by the owners themselves, not affiliated with this   document.

Table of Contents

Welcome

That long stare that you give yourself in the mirror each and every morning can be quite daunting after a while. The person that is staring back at you is asking, why are we doing this? Why do we get up at 0'dark thirty, Monday through Friday, and repeat the same tasks over and over again? Is it because you love repetition? Do you love the people that you get to interact with each day? I know what you are thinking. I know that in the back of your mind, you are telling yourself, right this very second, that you have to provide for your family. You have to feed them, cloth them and keep them healthy. These are your responsibilities as an adult, right? I get it. However, there is another side to this thought. The person that you are working for see's value in you. It is not the value that you are thinking of either. He/She may interact with you or laugh and joke around during the workday, but when it is all said and done, you hold a certain monetary value to that individual. That's what it boils down to. Looking at it that way makes it even more daunting, staring at your reflection in the mirror. There comes a time when we all will question ourselves as to why we aren't making ourselves happy.

Think about the following statement. I overheard a saying a while back and I couldn't tell you who said it, but it went something like "Take care of yourself first because if you were to die today, your job posting would be online before your obituary." That brings it into perspective right?

So, what can you do about it? How do you obtain freedom? How do you make a living for yourself? These questions have been asked over and over again throughout history. They have also been acted on over and over again. What do you think the driving force behind the "Gold Rush" in the late 1800's and early 1900's was? Most people will say that it was a chance to get rich by striking gold in "them there hills". However, all of those decisions came down to one single thought. How can I not be beholden to someone else? Entrepreneurship, at its base, is exactly that. You want to make your own money and not make it for someone else who will share a little sliver of it with you. You want to vacation when you want to and not have to ask that same person if it is ok. You want to implement your own strategies for how you will do business and not go along with what that same person is telling you. These are the core questions. If you want that type of freedom, you are probably an entrepreneur at heart.

Why is "Hustle and Grind" in the title of this book? I strategically placed that wording in there because, you as the reader, need to understand that in order to get where you want to be, you are going to have to work for it. You can't just come to the conclusion that you want to take my career advice and put the pieces together and just make money. That will not happen if you can't hustle. It will not happen if you can't grind it out. It will not be easy. You will question yourself often. However, your drive for setting this plan into motion should be more than enough to push through to achievement.

How do you hustle? Do you remember your high school days? Do you remember the football coach or your field hockey coach? Do you remember them "jumping into your shit" when you weren't moving fast enough? I do, all of the time. In this business, you have got to hustle. If you don't, you will fail. That is just the plain and simple truth of the matter. Set your monthly or quarterly goals regarding how much money you want to earn. Then find the opportunities that are going to meet those goals. Finally, implement a sourcing plan and recruiting plan to accomplish said goals. Later on in this book, you will discover how to source individuals and how to recruiting those individuals for the opportunities that you are contracted to fill.

The second piece of the puzzle here is the grind. The grind can be brutal on your mental capacity to be an entrepreneur. You will see the grind come into play when you are submitting really good qualified candidates for your job orders (opportunities) but they just aren't being selected for interviews or hires. You must go into this business with a mindset that this is going to happen. Your candidates will not always get hired. However, you keep grinding and submitting and eventually you will place the right candidate with the right opportunity.

WHAT IS RECRUITING?

Recruitment is the process of finding, screening, hiring and eventually onboarding job candidates. The recruitment process can be relatively straightforward, but advances in technology, a tight labour market and a workforce pool that might span five generations can make the first step -- finding potential candidates -- particularly challenging. Recruitment is a key part of human resource management (HRM). Skilled recruitment efforts will make a company stand out and be more attractive to potential employees, a strategy that can directly impact a company's bottom line.

How recruitment works

Once a job description has been established, HR or external recruitment agencies post the position on a wide variety of job sites and social media platforms, as well as notify existing employees on the company's intranet or web portal.

Resumes are submitted and screened. In some cases, recruiters will also solicit interest from people who have not submitted resumes, but whose work experience may fit the open job's □ualifications.

Next, potential candidates are interviewed and may be tested for drug and alcohol use. In addition, some companies are turning to artificial intelligence (AI)-powered screening tools to help more quickly identify potential candidates, assess strengths and weaknesses, and come up with questions that can speed the decision-making process. References are checked, and ultimately, the hiring manager or hiring team makes a choice. The new employee will then often go through an onboarding process to ensure an easy transition to the new role

Types of recruiting techniques

Although some companies still rely on a "We're Hiring" sign on the door, most companies tackle recruitment the way they do marketing -- with a multi-tiered approach. Recruitment marketing can include everything from promotion on social media to billboard ads, public relations (PR) campaigns and even bonuses to existing employees for successful candidate referrals.

Open positions are posted on more than job websites; Twitter, Facebook and LinkedIn are other popular choices. Ads on search engines that pop up in response to a query are another option. Large employers can also utilize other strategies, such as brand advertising, which showcases a company's benefits and perks and promotes culture and work styles. A strong Net Promoter Score (NPS) can also be highlighted. To attract certain groups of employees, such as millennials, a company may stress the value or importance of the work being done.

Why recruitment is important

Employees are the lifeblood of companies, so finding and attracting the best candidates possible is of utmost importance. A poor recruitment effort can result in unfilled jobs and a loss of revenue, while successful recruitment will bring in the right candidates on a timely basis, ensuring a business is able to continue to move forward.

Also, in a competitive hiring market, employee retention can be tricky, but an effective recruitment strategy can minimize that risk by ensuring the right people are hired into the right roles.

Sources of recruitment

When looking to fill open roles, employers have two options: Look internally, or hire from the outside. Both have advantages and disadvantages.

Internal candidates need little to no onboarding as they are familiar with the company, but moving an existing employee into a new role still leaves the old role to fill.

On the other hand, external candidates can bring fresh eyes, enthusiasm and skills to a company, but it is vital to ensure new employees will be a good fit in the company culture.

THE RECRUITING PROCESS

This is the process you should follow or closely adapt a similar process that works for you. I can tell you that this has worked for me in the past, therefore, I continue to follow it. It is important that you tweak this process to fit how you want to do business though.

1. <u>Finding opportunities (Job Orders)</u> It is very simple to find these opportunities because the internet job boards are littered with them. I challenge you to try this, right now, so that you can visually see what I am talking about. Open your browser and go to any of the Job Boards. i.e Indeed, Simply Hired, Monster, Career Builder etc.. Now, in the search bar, type in "Recruiter" and select the "Commission" icon or button to indicate that yo are looking for commission only opportunities. What comes up? How many 1099 contractor/commission only opportunities came up? Look for these Key Terms in the results: 1099 Recruiter, Remote Recruiter, and Contract Recruiter. Once you have identified these, screen through them to ensure that they are in fact 1099 opportunities. Remember, don't limit yourself to your locality. Leave the city/state

blank so you see all of the nationwide opportunities. As a recruiter, you don't have to live in the same area that you are recruiting for.

2. <u>Submit your tailored recruiting resume to them</u> – You may not get a call back on every single one that you attempt. However, keep in mind that there is a better chance of getting a signed IC agreement due to the fact that the individual/company that you are going to contract with doesn't lose anything by signing you. They have no skin in your game, remember? If you produce and make money, they make money. If you don't, they haven't lost anything. Remember that.

3. <u>Understand the candidates</u> – At this point, you really need to dissect the job order. When I say job order, I am referring to the candidates that the business that you are contracted with are looking for. Ask that business for a quick requisition for that will identify all of the criteria that they want in a candidate. How many years of experience and in what areas? What level of education do they want? Can education be supplemented with experience? Do they need any specific certifications or qualifications? Ensure that you know what they location is that you are hiring for. What is the pay rate or range of pay?

4. <u>Start sourcing candidates</u> – What is sourcing? This is just the recruiter term for finding people to submit. (Refer to the section on sourcing for a better understanding on how to do this and the tools available to you)

5. <u>Interview the candidates</u> – Once you have identified a pool of candidates that meet the qualifications set forth by the company you are working with, start interviewing them. This means scheduling a time with them and speaking with them about the opportunity that you have. Gauge the level of interested from the candidate. Ask them how dedicated they are to finding a new career position or making a move to another company? Validate what their resume as shown you. Talk to them about pay, benefits, and job responsibilities. You need to get a warm and fuzzy about submitting them to your point of contact at the business you are representing.

6. <u>Submitting your candidates</u> – So, you have sourced and interviewed numerous candidates. You have selected the best of the best from your candidate pool and are ready to send them to the company. How you do this will vary based on opportunities. One business might have you submit the resumes directly to the hiring manager via email. Other might have you facilitate a call

with the candidates so that the hiring manager can conduct a second interview. Some might even have a platform for you to submit to directly to an account manager. (This is popular with crowd-sourcing sites)

<u>Getting Paid</u>

We all want to get paid for our efforts right? That is why we are choosing this endeavor. There are a few different methods that you might be paid for these hires. Please keep in mind that not every candidate that you submit will get hired. The more you submit, the better your chances are for having one of your candidates selected for hire. Typically, most 1099 opportunities are going o pay a flat rate to a recruiter for the find. These rates will vary based on industry as well. It has been my experience that the range will go from $500.00 per hire to nearly $2500.00 per hire. The lower end of this spectrum is usually for your hard trades and skilled labor positions. The upper limit is generally your cleared Information Technology professionals. Keep in mind, these are my experiences. It is very possible to find opportunities that pay more or less. Another thing to think about is guarantee periods. This may create a delay in getting paid. One of the guidelines with the business that you are working with might be that the candidates that they hire must be working for a specified amount of time before they will pay the recruiter for the find. I have seen these go from 30 days to 90 days. Again, these are my experiences. Learn your abilities after you get started in this game. Figure out how much money you want to make each quarter or month. Then determine how many hires you will need and ultimately, how many people you will need to source to create those hires. It is thinking backwards to determine the outcome. Once you have done this for a while, you will see a trend in your ability and you will be able to more accurately assess your income potential.

WHAT IS AN INDEPENDENT CONTRACTOR?

Independent contractors, those mysterious workers who seem to have all the freedom in the world because they "work for themselves." Speaking from experience, it's not that glamorous. However, there are some advantages and disadvantages to contract work. You do have a lot of freedom in how you work. You also have a little more of a headache when it comes to paying your taxes, as well as ensuring consistency of income.

What Is An Independent Contractor?

An independent contractor is a person or entity contracted to perform work for—or provide services to—another entity as a nonemployee. As a result, independent contractors must pay their own Social Security and Medicare taxes. The payer must correctly classify each payee as either an independent contractor or employee. Another term for an independent contractor is a freelancer.

Understanding Independent Contractors

Doctors, dentists, veterinarians, lawyers, and many other professionals who provide independent services are classified as independent contractors by the Internal Revenue Service (IRS). However, the category also includes contractors, subcontractors, freelance writers, software designers, auctioneers, actors, musicians, and many others who provide independent services to the general public. Independent contractors have become increasingly prevalent in the rise of what has been dubbed "the gig economy."

Important: An independent contractor, or freelancer, is a person or entity contracted to perform work for—or provide services to—another entity as a nonemployee.

In the United States, independent contractors are considered sole proprietors or single-member limited liability companies (LLCs). They must report all their income and expenses on Schedule C of Form 1040 or Schedule E if they have profits or losses from rental properties. Further, they must submit self-employment taxes to the IRS, usually on a □uarterly basis using Form 1040-ES.

However, as sole proprietors, independent contractors do not necessarily pay taxes on their gross earnings. Applicable business expenses can reduce their overall tax obligation. The difference between gross earnings and business expenses is the net income, the amount on which taxes are due. As of 2019 independent contractors pay 12.4% in Social Security contributions and 2.9% in Medicare payments on the first $132,900 of their net income, plus 2.9% on their net income in excess of $132,900. Some independent contractors may also have to pay state sales taxes, depending on the product they are producing.

Independent contractors must keep track of their earnings and include every payment received from clients. Clients are legally obliged to issue 1099-Misc forms to their contractors if the amount they paid warrants that expense. If an independent contractor earns more than $599 from a single-payer, that payer is re□uired to issue the contractor a 1099 form detailing their earnings for the year.

Independent Contractor vs Employee

Workers can be classified as either an employee or an independent contractor. When a worker is an independent contractor, the employer can control only the □uality or result of the job—not the method through which the work is done. When the worker is an employee, the payer can mandate that the output occur in a particular place and at a certain time or pace. A business owner has more control over the completion of the job.

In return for this control over work specifics, the owner commits to provide the employee with several benefits. These include matching Social Security and Medicare contributions, providing the tools re□uired to complete the project, the potential of employer-sponsored retirement plans such as a 401(k) or IRA, and giving the worker access to a workplace.

In contrast, independent contractors must provide benefits for themselves, including paying both the employee and employer portions of Social Security and Medicare payments, among other expenses. The independent contractor must still meet the payer's □uality standard and time frame while producing the product. Independent contractors often work for employers who are physically far removed from their location. As such, they must be ready to compete in the global market for work. Being an independent contractor has downsides, as they have no access to unemployment insurance or workers' compensation payments.

WHY WORK FROM HOME? BENEFITS?

Let's be real, no matter where you're working from, you're still doing just that: working.

So, should you work from home or work from the office? It honestly comes down to the environment you'll be most effective in, along with the industry you're in. (And how nice your home office is.). With that said, let's take a look at some of the classic benefits of telecommuting!

Work in your PJs, avoid the commute, answer emails from a hammock while sipping a pineapple dai☐uiri—you've heard the common benefits of working remotely (and yes, they're true!). But there are some things that might surprise you about what it's like when you don't have to go into the office every day.

Working from home is not a new trend anymore. There are different pros and cons of working from home. In this chapter, I will share some of the major benefits of working from home.

Do remember working from home these days doesn't mean you are on your own. Many progressive companies now let their employees work from home, or they prefer hiring people (Freelancers, digital nomad, and others) who don't need office and love working from home.

Not all working from home is created e☐ual. Just ask Stanford University economics professor Nicholas Bloom. The abrupt spike in telecommuting during the coronavirus pandemic strikes him as a borderline crisis — for workers and for companies. He recently wrote that it is "creating a productivity hit to firms and a mental health hit to employees with costs for years to come."

Working from home during the coronavirus pandemic, though, shouldn't be conflated with the working from home Bloom recommends. This is crisis working from home — unplanned, government-mandated and coinciding with widespread school closures. Many people are working from their literal beds, with shoddy Wi-Fi and kids underfoot.

"For many of us, the current experience was like leaping from the plane after [five] minutes of sky-diving lessons," he wrote. "We just had to jump and hope."

One major advantage of working from home is you will save time on commuting from home to office. In major cities, this is a real-time burner. For example, where I come from, people spend more than 2 hours every day travelling from home to office and vice versa. Since I work from home, I end up saving 48 hours every month on commuting. Not to mention that I also save the hassle of getting stuck in traffic.

Another set of people working from home are bloggers, freelancers, entrepreneurs who are their boss, and many of them are usually in a dilemma to be working from home or renting out an office space. The reason they want an office space is that they feel it offers better productivity and discipline.

Well, this differs from person to person. For example, From last nine years, I mostly work from home and often when I get burned out or feel that working from home is not giving me productivity, I usually go to coworking spaces such as

Instaoffice, WeWork, MyHQ, 91Springboard & other cafes in my city.

Why should you do this?
Well, here are the reasons I can think of…

No one in their right mind would recommend this chaos — but just like Fifth Harmony, it shouldn't give all working from home a bad reputation. Here's how intentional, appropriately e☐uipped working from home can benefit employees and employers alike, according to three experts:

1. Your Office Can Be Any Kind
You'll probably work from home if you work remotely. But that doesn't mean you have to have filled a corner of your living room with a clunky desk, a huge monitor, and an ugly rolling chair. You can fit your office wherever it fits in your life. I've heard about a remote worker who uses her kitchen breakfast bar as a standing desk (all those health benefits with no investment!) and one who converted part of her bedroom closet into a "hidden" office so she can just shut her work away at the end of the day.

2. Your Office Can Be Anywhere—and I Mean Anywhere!

And you're not tied to your home, either. That doesn't mean your only other location will be the coffee shop around the corner: You can take care of your job while travelling (passengers only if you're in the car, please!), enjoying the great outdoors (thanks to long laptop battery life and tethering to your phone), or even listening to your favourite band at a live concert (a tested and true location of a remote customer service manager I know who's a die-hard country music fan).

3. You'll Save Money

Of course, you'll see an immediate difference in your bank account when you don't need to bear the costs of commuting. But you'll also find savings in other areas. You won't have to force yourself into a suit and polished shoes anymore if that's not your style—no more separate wardrobes for work and for the rest of your life! And you can also save on food costs since you'll easily be able to whip up your own lunch and coffee if you work from home.

4. Your Schedule Can Be Your Own

A lot of the work that can be done remotely nowadays can also be done on a flexible schedule. For example, if you're a web developer or a content creator, you can most likely do your coding or writing whenever it suits you as long as you meet your deadlines. So, night owls, rejoice! You can still put in your eight hours without starting at 8 AM.

If you do need to work specific hours, you're sure to have still some break time—time you can use however you'd like! Even if you have just 10 minutes, you can do something that just wouldn't be possible in a traditional office: bust those samba moves, play a few tunes on your guitar, or take a refreshing power nap. You're guaranteed to come back, feeling more refreshed than you would after 10 minutes at your desk surfing Facebook.

5. You Can Learn More and Become More Independent

Because you don't have colleagues just a few feet away or a tech team one floor down, you'll find yourself developing the skill of looking for your own answers and becoming more proactive to find what you need on your own. Of course, you can still ask questions and get help if you need to. But, a lot of the time, you can do a Google search, download a free guide, or check out your company's wiki to find the answer yourself just as □uickly.

And you'll also end up with some skills simply because you need them to work well remotely. For example, you'll probably notice that you're writing more clear and concise emails and being more sensitive to your team's different schedules out of necessity once you've worked remotely for a while. Not bad things to be good at!

6. You Can Actually Have Enjoyable and Effective Meetings

I bet you don't know anyone who enjoys meetings. (No amount of free coffee and doughnuts can make up for having to sit in a stuffy conference room next to the pen-clicking guy from sales!) When you work remotely, you'll not only be able to choose your breakfast and your seat, but you can also be much more effective. With just a few clicks, you can have ten people on a video call that'll probably last just 15 minutes instead of 45. And you can use the chat function in the video call to □uickly share docs (forget making copies or having everyone search their emails) or to add important comments without interrupting anyone.

7. You Can Keep in Touch More Easily—and Maybe Have Some Fun Doing It!

Most people are afraid that they'll be lonely or left out when they work remotely. But the opposite is usually true, as there's a huge range of communication tools for remote workers available now. Some will even let you have a little fun together with features like emojis, chat room "bots," or silly effects in video chats. With them, you can celebrate a colleague's birthday by putting on a virtual top hat and monocle in your Google Hangout instead of suffering through an out-of-tune round of "Happy Birthday" and a grocery store cake!

8. You Can Keep in Touch More Effectively

Because you don't have everyone physically around you all the time, you become much more aware of the importance of keeping in touch. Instead of just knowing that you can pop around the corner to chat with Rena about the site redesign whenever you like, you know that you need to write her or at least have a video chat. So, either in the process of composing your message or planning the meeting, you'll refine your thoughts and □uestions and end up saving time for both of you when you do have that discussion.

9. You Can Stay More Focused

With some willpower and a steady routine, you'll soon learn to avoid being distracted by the TV or your next load of laundry. And, in fact, you should find yourself getting more done when you work remotely. That's because you can control your working situation much more—you don't have to worry about co-workers stopping by to "just ask a □uick □uestion" (and 20 minutes later...), obligatory socializing when you grab more coffee or offending someone by shutting the door to your office. When you're remote and need to really concentrate, you can just change your status in the group chat to "do not disturb" and buckle down.

10. You Can Avoid Office Politics

There's the old saying about relatives that "You can't choose your family," and the same goes for your co-workers. You might not be best friends with everyone when you work remotely. But, because idle chatting and time just hanging around the break room aren't possible, remote workers tend to skip the gossiping and posturing that happens in traditional work settings. And that's a huge bonus for everyone involved, isn't it?

THOUGHTS ON YOU WORKING FOR YOU

If you are reading this book, you are either intrigued or you have made a decision. That decision is based on the fact that you are tired of working yourself to death and having someone else take all of the profits from your efforts. As a Recruiter, I work in my own office, located in my own home, near all of the amenities that make my life easier. One of the greatest factors of working from home is the lifestyle. I will tell you exactly what I need to be successful. I need my laptop, internet connection and my cell phone. That's it! I need to be able to look at the job descriptions of the positions that I need to fill and bounce those requirements off of resumes that I have sourced from people either looking for work or enticing someone to take a chance on another position, otherwise known as headhunting. Now, I can be successful at this either in my home office or on the beach. I can be poolside or out with friends. You just have to have the discipline to do the work. That is the only way you will get paid in this business. Lifestyle, Lifestyle, Lifestyle!!!!!

On the flip side of the idea of lifestyle, keep in mind that it is also about work during odd times. Recruiting never stops. You get out of it what you put into it. If you half ass your effort, you will get half assed results. You can't approach this type of work with a lazy attitude. You can't work a few hours per day and expect to make a good living. Working as a recruiter is a process driven environment. There are steps that you will follow with slight variations depending on who you are contracted to work for. I lay out an entire chapter in this book as a guide so that you can keep yourself on track. It really boils down to being a disciplined, goal driven entrepreneur. That's right! In this line of work, you are an entrepreneur. You need to realize that you are working for you. Roughly five years ago, I had to have a heart to heart conversation with myself. You see, I am also a Real Estate Agent in my local community. However, keep in mind, that this was prior to me discovering what being an independent contractor was really about. When I decided to sell real estate, I really didn't understand the entrepreneurial concept. I approached it as having a boss and reporting my results to the broker. I quickly found out that no one really cared if I was successful or a failure. The reason being is that the broker didn't have any skin in my game. If I produced, he made some money. However, if I didn't produce, he lost nothing.

What I am getting at here is that you need to recognize that you are working for you and no one else. Remember this concept because as you start this endeavor, you will undoubtedly question your ability and feel lost. However, as you work through these issues, your own systems and processes will become clear and you will find that you can make money and only be accountable to yourself.

THE DIFFERENT FREELANCE PLATFORMS

If you are a freelancer looking for work, you probably know how exhausting the task can be. However, there are freelance websites dedicated to helping professionals like yourself find work. In this chapter, we will list the best freelance websites on the internet.

Where can you get the ideal work or client? If you're a freelancer, we can help point you in the right direction.

We know that freelance work has its perks, and searching for customers isn't one of them. Marketing your services is indeed one of the most tedious tasks that you can face. This is where freelance websites come in.

However, websites offering freelance work come at varying degrees of reach, work types, and payment terms. If you're not careful, you can end up wasting time, effort, and, worse, money on platforms with ⬜uestionable standing.

That's why we came up with these best freelance websites for beginners and professionals, so you can weed out undesirables and focus on the most reliable ones. After all, time is money. Below, you'll find it easy to compare the similarities and, more importantly, differences between each platform. Key features to consider include job types, payment terms, and communication channels.

Freelancers looking to earn more money now have more options than ever before. Whether you are freelancing full-time, looking to earn some pound or dollar on the side, or are looking for a freelancer to help you do some work, these are some of the best freelance websites that you should be considering in 2020.

Of course, there are many different factors that make a website great for freelancers. They can range from the number and variety of jobs available for freelancers, the fre□uency that new opportunities are presented, and of course one of the most important factor - how diligent they are when it comes to paying for your services.

Be safe in the knowledge that the best freelance websites that we have rounded up below tick these boxes. Let's check them out.

Using a freelance website is great for those searching for additional ways to earn extra money, those who simply enjoy the freedom of freelancing, and those who want to gain more development professionally. Millions of individuals are reaping the benefits of professional freelancing, just as the digital nomad lifestyle rises in popularity. Sure, you can pick up a guide on how to land great freelancing gigs, but it's so much more than simply signing up on popular platforms. Whether you are working on location or remotely, there are options for anyone in almost any trade to find freelance work. Once you've established a good portfolio, there are some great websites that you can find work as a freelancer. Sometimes, the platform will even provide all of the tools that are needed to develop your portfolio so that clients are attracted to it.

What Are Freelance Websites?

Freelance websites are platforms, where both people looking for work and employers post their offers.

Being a freelancer is an excellent way to turn your talent or hobby into money. You have the freedom to apply for only the projects that you like, or you're good at.

Needless to say, using these websites will help you set a solid start for your freelance career. They'll assist you in finding first clients easily and earning employers trust along the way.

Also, you constantly sharpen your skill by taking different projects from various employers. In the end, your portfolio shall grow, and there will be many more job offers.

1. Fiverr

freelancer can showcase finished projects to the public so potential clients can easily pick someone whose creation sparks their interest. It's an alternative that removes the need to contact workers one by one.

What is more, Fiverr offers you free learning courses to develop your skills and teach you how to pitch to clients.

2. Upwork

Upwork offers tools to kickstart your freelance journey – collaborative space, built-in invoice maker, and transparent recruitment process. You might also be able to work for many famous clients such as Microsoft, Airbnb, Dropbox, etc.

Anyone who is looking for flexibility in their jobs should definitely check this freelance website.

3. Toptal

Toptal is a freelance website which promises companies they can hire the top 3% of global freelancers. Surely, you can be one of them if you work hard enough in building your skills.

4. Simply Hired

One of the best things about Simply Hired is that you can browse freelance jobs in your nearby location. Additionally, there is a list of top salaries and a tool to estimate your fee. This is helpful to benchmark for a specific work you want to do.

You'll also be able to create a resume from the website and learn many things from their blog.

5. PeoplePerHour

This freelance website has over 1.5 million freelancers that used their service. Every worker will have a rating, which is a great promotion.

People Per Hour is free for freelancers, but the competition can be very challenging. You should always improve and set a reasonable fee so you'll be more likely to get hired.

6. A□uent

A□uent has won many awards as a freelancing firm. The freelance website is well-established and known to deliver high-□uality workers for creative, digital, and marketing purposes.

While Aquent states that they mainly accept someone who has 2+ years of working experience, fresh graduates are still welcome to explore their available jobs. And if you doubt how much your skill is worth, there is a salary guide to help you set your price.

7. Crowded

Crowded boasts it's AI-powered recruitment process that will find the most suitable applicants for companies. This freelance website will rank everyone based on their price, experience, and skills.

The feature is also great for workers so that they don't have to apply to each job opening manually. Just let the algorithm do the work and then wait for the call from the employer.

8. The Creative Group

The freelance website makes it easy for freelancers out there to find a job they want. TCG, as it's called, allows you to upload a resume or a LinkedIn profile to start looking for a job.

Once there is an opportunity that suits your interest, you can try to apply for the job.

9. 99Designs

This freelance website aims to focus on designer jobs – everything from logos to book covers. It also allows clients to start a contest that everyone in 99Designs can participate in.

At zero cost, you'll get a platform to showcase your work and improve your creative knowledge with its up-to-date articles.

10. Nexxt

Nexxt categorizes the jobs search according to 4 criteria: career focus, local focus, diversity focus, and global focus. The third one is beneficial to accommodate a more inclusive work environment for everyone.

With these categories, this freelance website also enables you to try various freelance jobs that align with your career path.

11. Writer Access

If you want to become a freelance writer, Writer Access is the best platform. It covers all kinds of writing jobs, including online articles, case studies, tech papers, etc.

This freelance website many tools such as content analytics, keyword optimization, and content planner to get more work done efficiently.

12. TaskRabbit

House-related freelance jobs in TaskRabbitNot all freelancing jobs are digital. TaskRabbit is a freelance website that focuses on housework.

Be it furniture assembling, moving and packing, plumbing, or anything else – you can find it on TaskRabbit.

13. Skyword

Loads of content marketing vacancies can be easily found here. You can register to work as a freelance content strategist, editorial manager, and so on.

Furthermore, it doesn't just serve US or English-only companies because Skyword has been trusted by clients from 27 countries with 13 languages support.

14. Designhill

This freelance website offers a transparent price upfront so clients can anticipate how much the finished design can cost. It's a pretty useful feature as there is so many design work with different prices.

15. Freelancer

This freelance website is the largest crowdsourcing marketplace, with 32 million registered users. To match that number, there are of thousands of jobs that you can opt as a freelance worker.

You can register here for free and with hundreds of vacancies posted every day.

16. Guru

After you sign up, you will be a part of 3 million freelancers across the globe in search of various jobs, such as web development, writing, architecture, and so on.

17. Hireable

Hireable nearby job searchHireable gives you an opportunity to get a freelance job outside America or Europe with e☐ual opportunity.

It has a straightforward user interface and provides exactly what you expect from a freelance website: you get job alerts, recommendations, and see your saved jobs as well as the jobs you applied for.

18. FlexJobs

FlexJobs doesn't only provide a platform for freelance work, but it also encourages everyone to try this career path. Furthermore, the freelance website collects jobs from around the world.

At $14.95 a month, you get full access to its wide network of employers, various skill tests, and detailed description of every company.

Being a freelancer means that you have more flexibility in choosing your next job while having the freedom of when and where to do it.

To help you realize your new career path, we have listed the best freelance websites for you. Here is a brief overview of some of the best:

- ✓ Upwork is the overall best freelance website that has tools to support your career development.
- ✓ You should check Designhill if you're a designer.
- ✓ Skyword is a global crowdsourcing platform that fits freelance content and marketing workers.
- ✓ TaskRabbit opens up possibilities outside digital professions with its house-related freelance jobs.
- ✓ WriterAccess makes it easy for everyone who loves writing to make money out of it.
- ✓ Freelancer offers the largest network of remote jobs.
- ✓ Join Aquent if you're already an experienced worker because the platform is made specifically for professionals.
- ✓ Nexxt provides a more diverse and inclusive platform for everyone with a different background to start looking for freelance jobs.
- ✓ With Fiverr, you can look for a job while still be able to improve your skill with its free online courses.
- ✓ Toptal gives you a high reward if you have grown your portfolio enough by offering your service as "the top 3% of global talent."

SOURCING

Sourcing tools are one of the most important aspects of recruiting. You might be able to act in an account manager role all day long, speaking to business owners about using your skill set to fill their vacant jobs. However, if you can't fill those roles, you will not be in the recruiting game very long. The following section outlines my sourcing strategies and what I use to ensure that my requisitions do not go un-filled. Some of these are free to use and others are not. It is important to weight the Return on Investment (ROI) when looking at purchasing tools. You can get started using free tools though. Keep that in mind.

<u>The Job Boards</u>

There are many job boards out there for you to scour through endless resumes. Indeed, for example will allow you to search free resumes with keywords. There is a catch though. If you use the free tools on Indeed, you will see the information on the resume but you will not be able to see the name or any of the contact information. *I would urge you to read the "Boolean Search" portion of this book, for a nice work around on that. There are other job boards that are good as well. Monster, Career Builder and others have the same basic functionality. You can use a combination of the free job boards, social media and Boolean searches to find the people that you are targeting. You can also pay for the job board information. I know that Indeed is a great source if you are planning on paying for the service. So, for a few dollars, you can get the information pretty quickly. Again, you have to weigh the ROI.

Social Media

This is probably my favorite way to source new candidates. There are so many platforms that you can freely post Job Descriptions to and get quick responses. The idea is to build a nice candidate pool. If you do this first, you have available candidates to fill requisitions quickly, making you look better. Personally, when I decided that social media was going to be my main platform, I started building my presence. Let me give you LinkedIn for example. When I started my LinkedIn account, I be-friended about twenty people. These were people that I knew. I didn't stop there. I currently have nearly 7,000 1st connections on LinkedIn. When I post a Job that needs to be filled, tens of thousands of people see it daily. So, how did I build my LinkedIn presence? It will sound a little un-orthodox. Every time I found myself sitting in the bathroom, I just took the suggested friends list and friended them all. I repeated this over and over again. Before I knew it, I had a pretty good following.

<u>**Referrals**</u>

Once you establish yourself in this industry, candidates should be coming to you. You should have helped so many people in numerous different fields that they refer their friends and family to you. They do this because they know that you will take care of their family as you did them. Working in this industry for nearly fifteen years has taught me that the constant asking for referrals will do wonders for your future gigs. I have to stress this point one more time. When you are helping a candidate get into the position that they want, ask them for a referral. You may not get one from then at that exact moment but in a few years when their sister or brother or close friend is in need, they will call on you and they will remember what you did for them.

IDENTIFYING LUCRATIVE EMPLOYMENT MARKETS?

You are an entrepreneur, and your company is you. Your paycheck is the revenue generated from the services you provide your employer. Like any successful business, you want to maximize your revenues and retain the customer – in this case, your employer. This is achieved by providing high-□uality service and charging a fee that is competitive and worthy of the value provided. Put simply, you want to get paid what you are worth.

To accurately assess your fair market value, start with reliable employer-reported pay data like that found on some websites and follow these three steps:

1. Match your job description to a benchmark job
2. Assess employer factors
3. Evaluate your performance and compensable attributes

Match Your Job Description

The first step is to match your job description to a benchmark job. A common mistake that many people make is trying to compare their value based on a job title alone.

The problem with trying to match pay to job titles is that titles and their associated responsibilities are not always consistent across companies. Matching the only title, you may find yourself comparing your salary to people performing completely different jobs.

When trying to align your job description with a "benchmark" job, a minimum 70 per cent match of your job responsibilities to the benchmark description, you are trying to match is recommended. If you intend to present your findings to your employer, use employer-reported that has been matched on job descriptions and considers factors that actually influence pay, such as a job's responsibilities and required skills.

Your manager will likely check the source of the data, which is where the difference between employer-reported and self-reported data (from employees) really matters. In fact, a recent survey concluded that 95% of employers do not trust self-reported data and more than 75% will not negotiate salary based on self-reported data because they believe it is less accurate and less carefully matched than employer-reported data.

When you speak to your manager, he or she may want to know more about your process for determining the benchmark job description and may have his or her own input. This should be considered a positive development. By discussing your job responsibilities and job level, both you and your boss will gain a better understanding of what needs to be done for you to succeed in your current position and earn your next promotion.

When you speak to your manager, he or she may want to know more about your process for determining the benchmark job description and may have his or her own input. This should be considered a positive development. By discussing your job responsibilities and job level, both you and your boss will gain a better understanding of what needs to be done for you to succeed in your current position and earn your next promotion.

For example, you may think that you are performing your position at a senior level (called Level III by Some websites, but perhaps "Senior" or "Experienced" by your employer); meanwhile, your manager is evaluating you at a middle level (Level II). By discussing this with your manager, you may have a "meeting of the minds" and you may become eligible not only a raise but also a promotion. If your manager disagrees, you will now have a clear idea of what it will take to get the next promotion. Don't be discouraged – this is really an opportunity for you to shine.

Assess Employer Factors

Salaries vary across locations, industries, and company sizes. Salaries are also affected by the job's position within the company pecking order: the number of people a job may supervise and the role of the job's supervisor. As a rule, larger companies pay their employees more than smaller companies because larger companies have greater spheres of influence and higher revenues per employee. Larger companies also tend to generate greater productivity and efficiency per worker. The trade-off is that small companies offer more direct access and exposure to senior-level executives, and sometimes offer a better professional experience. These factors must be considered if you are to assess your market value with your current employer accurately.

The industry you work in may also have a significant impact on the final value of your job. More profitable industries can afford to pay more and be more demanding at the same time. It is a widely observed trend that biotechnology employees typically earn more than their counterparts in manufacturing, who, in turn, earn more than those at non-profit and government organizations.

Again, if you intend to present your findings to your manager, using employer-reported data will lend greater credibility because it accounts for all the company factors that influence pay. Meanwhile, self-reported data provides minimal consideration to company, industry and geographic factors.

Having benchmarked your job, and accounted for employer factors, you should also assess how your performance and personal attributes impact your salary value. You must be realistic and practical when evaluating your own worth to an employer. All relevant skills, education, professional experience and past performance should be considered when trying to determine your final value.

When you are new to a position, you are likely to have some of the re□uired skills but may still be developing others. Conversely, if you are a seasoned veteran, you are likely to have all skills required by the job and are performing the job more efficiently than a recent hire. This increases your worth.

In addition to assessing your proficiency and job skills, your valuation should also consider how the less tangible elements of job performance—like attitude, teamwork, punctuality, education and certifications—increase your value. If you have attributes that are important to the company's success and they are in high demand, then you can expect higher pay. For example, a specialized technician at a chemical plant plays a pivotal role in keeping the plant running properly. The technician's employer may decide to pay above the average market value to avoid losing rare skills critical to the employer's success.

Calculating your final worth

After completing a thorough analysis of your worth, you can make the best assessment of your current pay. If your pay seems fair, you can focus on setting the goals that will signal that you are preparing yourself for your next promotion. If you are underpaid, it may be time to present your findings to your manager and ask for an explanation of your employer's pay practices. The objective is not to present an ultimatum, but rather to understand your employer's pay philosophy and to provide your employer with your research so that you together may discuss your performance and pay. There will be details to work through, but you will have opened the discussion and built a strong case for a pay raise and possible promotion.

CONDUCTING A BOOLEAN SEARCH?

n Monday, we (along with Google) celebrated the 200th birthday of a very special man – Mr George Boole. George Boole was a British mathematician whose work on logic laid many of the foundations for the digital revolution. His legacy was Boolean logic, a theory of mathematics in which all variables are either "true" or "false", or "on" or "off". This logic still underpins all digital devices, existing in almost every line of computer code, and it just so happens to be the means by which recruiters everywhere search for candidates on the likes of LinkedIn today.

Boolean search writing is a skill that top recruiters need to know directly in order to get meaningful candidate search results from a wide range of software, and is, therefore, a core skill you need to develop if you wish to be a successful recruiter. However, fully constructed Boolean search strings can look both confusing and complex, and therefore, difficult to write. But don't worry, because they aren't! And we're going to teach you why they aren't today.

What is Boolean Search?

Boolean Search is a way to organize your search using a combination of keywords and the three main Boolean operators (AND, OR and NOT), to produce more accurate and more relevant results for your candidate searches on LinkedIn and beyond.

The first important thing to appreciate about Boolean is that there are only five elements of syntax to understand. These are:

- ✓ AND
- ✓ OR
- ✓ NOT
- ✓ ()
- ✓ ""

By applying these appropriately, along with the keywords you wish to consider, you can create a huge range of search operations. There is no limit to how often you can use any of these elements in a search, so you can create very specific search strings, which will save you a lot of time in filtering the results.

The AND Operator

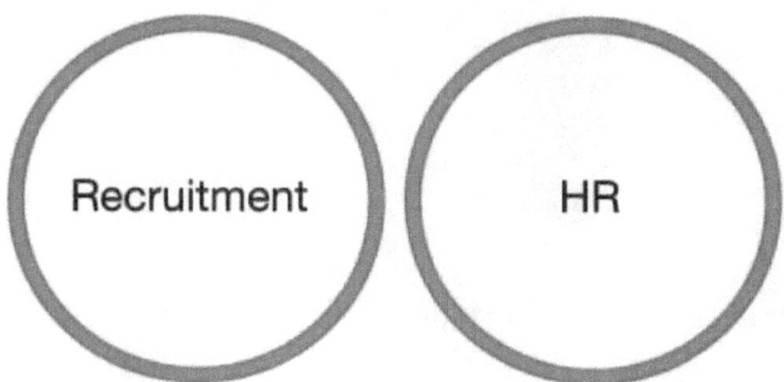

Take these two groups. In the first group are all the people who have the keyword "recruitment" somewhere in their LinkedIn profile. In the second, are all the people who have the keyword "HR" somewhere in their LinkedIn profile. When we use the Boolean string:

Recruitment AND HR

We are asking the LinkedIn database to search for all of the people who include both the word "recruitment" and the word "HR" on their LinkedIn profile. Meaning we are only looking to find candidates who fall in the cross-section of the Venn diagram – candidates who have both keywords mentioned in their profile:

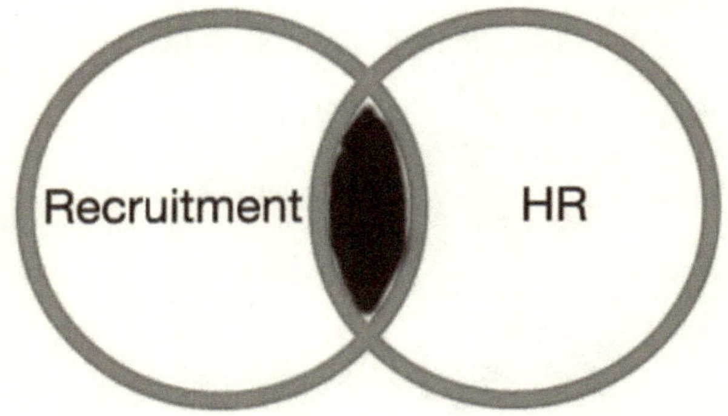

The more criteria we add using the AND operator, the fewer people we will find with our search, because by using AND we are narrowing our search. However, the people we do find from our search will be more relevant, as they will possess both of those skills.

The OR Operator

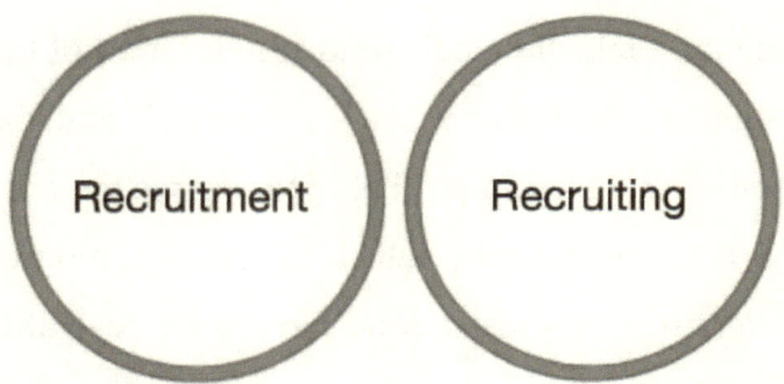

In this example, one group of people have the keyword "Recruitment" in their LinkedIn profile, while the other has the keyword "Recruiting". Both words mean exactly the same thing to you and I and anyone using either of the two terms to describe their job function or skillset on LinkedIn possessing exactly the same skillset, but to an electronic database, they are totally separate terms. When we use the Boolean string:

Recruitment OR Recruiting

We are asking the database to search for candidates who include either of the two terms in their LinkedIn profile, or both terms simultaneously. Meaning we are looking to find candidates who fall in either side of the Venn diagram or indeed, the cross-section:

Therefore, by using OR we are broadening/expanding our search to encompass profiles that have one result or the other or both.

Using OR enables us to find hidden talent, e.g. people who have expressed their skills and experience in a different way than you might normally search, e.g. banking OR bank OR finance OR financial, because by using OR we are broadening our search.

The Not Operator

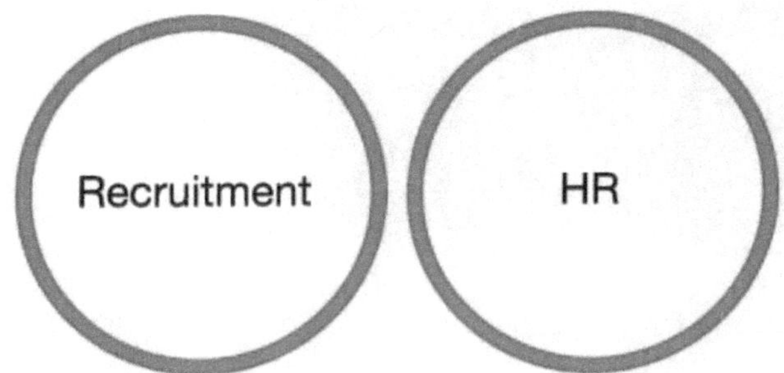

Like in the first example we used, one group of people have the keyword "Recruitment" in their LinkedIn profile, while the other has the keyword "HR". When we use the Boolean string:

Recruitment NOT HR

We are asking the database to search for candidates who have the word "Recruitment" in their profile but to exclude any candidates that also have the word "HR" in their profile and those who just have the word "HR" in their profile. Meaning we are looking to find candidates who fall just on the right-hand side of the Venn diagram:

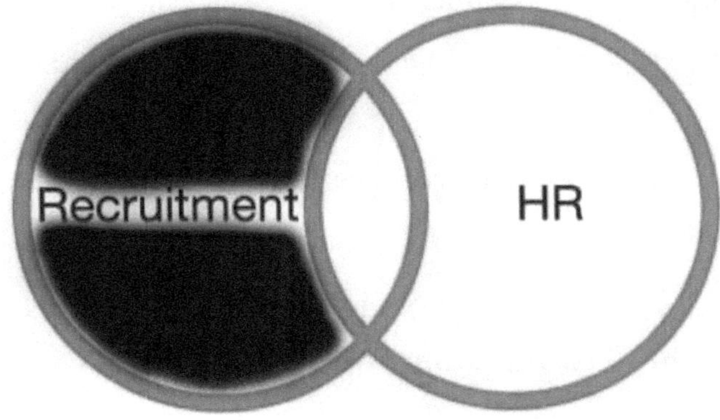

Using NOT enables us to remove false positives from our candidate searches, as by using NOT we are filtering our search and removing irrelevant results:

REMEMBER: Each of the 3 Boolean operators should always be written in UPPER CASE. If not, they will not work.

Brackets ()

When using a Boolean search, there is no way to determine how the computer will solve our equation. This means that in order to get the most relevant result for us, we have to use something called parentheses to tell the computer what to solve first. This is where using brackets comes into our Boolean search.

Using brackets is essential for writing complex search strings, but it can be their application that causes the most confusion amongst recruiters. Essentially, a clause within brackets is given priority over other elements around it. For example, if I was given the following search:

talent OR hr AND recruitment

Do I mean to say I want to find someone who has either the keyword "talent" or the keyword "HR" on their profile and has the word "recruitment" too? Or do I mean that they have to have "talent" or the combination of "HR" and "recruitment"? You see, the absence of brackets makes it impossible for the database to know what you mean. Watch how the meaning changes when you add brackets.

In the following example, I have told the database that I need to find someone who has either "talent" or "HR" or both, and that they also need to have "recruitment":

(talent OR hr) AND recruitment

But in the following example, I have told the database that I need to find someone who has "talent" or a combination of "recruitment" and "HR":

talent OR (hr AND recruitment)

The most commonplace that brackets are applied by recruiters is in the use of OR strings. Basically, if you've written OR somewhere in your search, think about where the brackets will go because their placement will affect how the computer solves your Boolean search □uery, which will affect search results you receive back.

Quotations ""

When using Boolean search, if the keyword you're searching for needs to be considered as a whole word, e.g. Gas Engineer, then it must be enclosed within quotation marks in your Boolean search string. If not, the database will consider the space between the two words to be an AND and will search the database for two terms – gas

AND engineer – and not what you want to search for which is the exact phrase "Gas Engineer".

In other words, you must use quotations wherever you have two or more words as a phrase in your Boolean search string that you know for certain should be right beside one another like "Information Technology" or "Human Resources", as □uotations define a number of words as one exact term.

Today, we've explained the basics of Boolean – the bread and butter if you will – which I hope helped you gain a better understanding of the fundamentals of Boolean search and made it less daunting to tackle in the future. There are, of course, several other Boolean modifiers you can use to refine further and improve your Boolean searches, as well as many more rules for the use of Boolean in various other search engines and databases beyond LinkedIn.

IN THE END

<u>Putting it all together (Step by Step)</u>

1. Take a look at yourself in the mirror. Determine right then, in that very moment, if you have the drive and determination to go out into the world and take what you can. If you can't say that for sure, please revisit this in a few years, when you again say, "Why am I not doing this myself".

2. Decide by which method you are going to implement these fundamentals. Are you going to start your own one person agency and start building your clientele? Will you just target those 1099 roles that you find on the job boards? Will it be a combination of both? If you are new to recruiting, I would advise that you start with the 1099 Independent Contractor roles first. If you are seasoned, maybe you should start that agency, develop a pricing plan to beat your competition and start developing accounts.

3. Start your Hustle and Grind and don't look behind. The future is now.

Do Not Go Yet; One Last Thing To Do

If you enjoyed this book or found it useful, I'd be very grateful if you'd post a short review on Amazon. Your support really does make a difference, and I read all the reviews personally so I can get your feedback and make this book even better.

Thanks again for your support!

www.ingramcontent.com/pod-product-compliance
Lightning Source LLC
Chambersburg PA
CBHW031422160726
47993CB00003B/1356